BOLIVIA

BOLIVIA

Karen Schimmel

CHELSEA HOUSE PUBLISHERS
New York Philadelphia

COVER: Two women and a child, dressed in traditional garb, take time out from selling vegetables at a street market in La Paz, Bolivia.

Chelsea House Publishers
Editor-in-Chief: Remmel Nunn
Managing Editor: Karyn Gullen Browne
Copy Chief: Juliann Barbato
Picture Editor: Adrian G. Allen
Art Director: Maria Epes
Deputy Copy Chief: Mark Rifkin
Assistant Art Director: Loraine Machlin
Manufacturing Manager: Gerald Levine
Systems Manager: Rachel Vigier
Production Manager: Joseph Romano

Places and Peoples of the World
Editorial Director: Rebecca Stefoff

Staff for BOLIVIA
Associate Editor: Kevin Bourke
Copy Editor: Philip Koslow
Editorial Assistant: Marie Claire Cebrián
Picture Researcher: Diana Gongora
Designer: Donna Sinisgalli

First Printing

1 3 5 7 9 8 6 4 2

Library of Congress Cataloging-in-Publication Data
Schimmel, Karen.
Bolivia/Karen Schimmel.
p. cm.—(Places and peoples of the world)
Summary: Examines the history, geography, people, economy,
and culture of Bolivia.
1. Bolivia—Juvenile literature. [1. Bolivia.] I. Title.
F3308.5.S35 1990   89-71256   CIP
984—dc20   AC
ISBN 0-7910-1109-7

CONTENTS

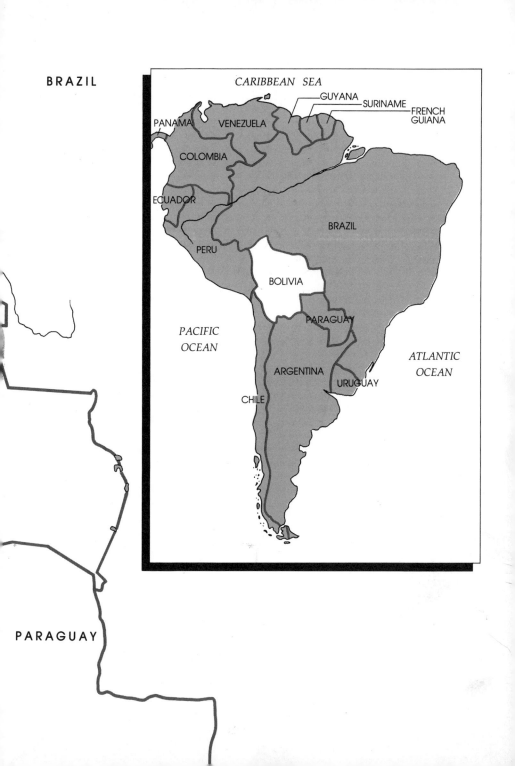

FACTS AT A GLANCE

Land and People

Area	424,162 square miles (1,111,304 square kilometers)
Highest Point	Mount Sajama, 21,391 feet (6,482 meters)
Major Rivers	Madre de Dios, Beni, Mamoré, Guaporé, Pilcomayo, Desaguadero
Major Lakes	Titicaca, Poopó
Constitutional Capital	Sucre (population 80,000)
Seat of Government	La Paz (population 955,000)
Major Cities	La Paz, Santa Cruz (population 419,000), Cochabamba (population 304,000), Oruro (population 132,000), Potosí (population 103,000)
National Population	6,876,000
Population Density	16 people per square mile (6 per square kilometer)
Population Distribution	Rural, 51 percent; urban, 49 percent
Official Languages	Spanish, Quechua, Aymara
Literacy Rate	64 percent

Ethnic Groups	Quechua, 30 percent; mestizo, 30 percent; Aymara, 25 percent; Caucasian, 14 percent; small Indian groups, Asians, and Arabs, 1 percent
Religions	Roman Catholic, 95 percent; Protestants and practitioners of traditional Indian beliefs, 5 percent
Average Life Expectancy	Men, 48.6 years; women, 53.0 years

Economy

Chief Exports	Tin, natural gas, antimony, gold, silver, tungsten, timber, coffee, beef, sugar
Chief Imports	Heavy machinery, transportation equipment, foodstuffs, clothing, household goods
Chief Agricultural Products	Potatoes, coffee, timber, beef, sugar, soybeans, barley, cocoa, rice, corn, bananas, citrus fruits, coca
Industries	Textiles, food processing, mining, clothing
Currency	Peso boliviano, divided into 100 centavos
Average Annual Income	Equal to U.S. $400

Government

Form of Government	Multiparty republic with 2 legislative houses (the Senate, with 27 members, and the Chamber of Deputies, with 157 members)
Head of State	President, elected to a four-year term
Local Government	Nine regional departments, divided into 98 provinces and 1,272 cantons; the heads of the departments and provinces are appointed by the president; mayors and councils of cities are elected by popular vote
Voting Rights	All married citizens at age 18, unmarried citizens at age 21

HISTORY AT A GLANCE

about 100 B.C. The Tiahuanaco culture first appears on the altiplano. It reaches its peak around A.D. 900.

A.D. 1200 The Tiahuanaco culture disappears. The Aymara kingdoms emerge as independent but loosely allied states.

mid-15th century Quechua Indians of the Inca empire venture south from what is now Peru to conquer the Indians of the altiplano.

1532 Francisco Pizarro lands at Tumbes, on the northern coast of Peru. He captures the Inca emperor Atahuallpa and eventually executes him. The Inca empire falls to the Spanish in late 1533.

1538 Spain's first two settlements in Upper Peru (as Bolivia was called) are founded at Chuquisaca and Porco.

1545 Silver is discovered at Potosí.

1561 Conquistadores traveling west from the Atlantic Ocean establish the town of Santa Cruz in what is now the southeastern Oriente region.

1650–1750	A decline in the output of silver at Potosí brings on a century-long depression from which Upper Peru never totally recovers.
1780	Indians led by Tupac Amarú attempt to expel the Spaniards from the altiplano and restore Inca rule; the Spanish destroy the rebellion.
1809	Bolivians set up an independent government and declare their freedom from Spanish rule. Independence fighters led by Pedro Domingo Murillo rebel in La Paz and throughout the altiplano.
1825	Upper Peru gains its independence, and the Republic of Bolivia is founded. Simón Bolívar writes the nation's first constitution.
1826	Antonio José de Sucre is elected Bolivia's first president.
mid- to late 19th century	A series of military governments gain control of the presidency by means of coups d'état.
1879	Bolivia and Chile go to war, and Bolivia is forced to give up its Pacific coastline to Chile.
1883	Bolivia's first political party, the Liberal party, is formed, heralding 50 years of civilian rule.
1899	La Paz is made the seat of the national government. Sucre remains the judicial and legal capital.
late 19th century	Tin replaces silver as the country's most important mine product.
early 20th century	Workers unite to form labor unions, and the first stirrings of a labor movement are felt.
1932	Bolivian troops seize several Paraguayan forts in the Gran Chaco region, touching off the Chaco War. More than 65,000 Bolivians die in the 3 years of fighting.
1936	The army overthrows civilian president José Luis Tejada Sorzano and replaces him with Colonel David Toro.

1941   A party called the Movimiento Nacionalista Revolucionario (MNR) is founded by a group of Bolivian intellectuals who support state ownership of the mines.

1943   The MNR and the military unite to oust the civilian president and install Major Gualberto Villarroel as the country's leader.

1952   After being denied the presidency in the election of 1951, the MNR stages a national revolution with the aid of the workers and Indians. A few months later, President Víctor Paz Estenssoro turns the country's three largest mining firms over to the newly created state-run mining corporation.

1953   The revolutionary government passes the Agrarian Reform Law, which turns much of the land held by the large landholders over to the Indians.

1964   Air Force general René Barrientos Ortuño overthrows the MNR government and declares himself president. Military leaders rule Bolivia for the next 18 years.

1982   Military rule ends as civilian president Hernán Siles Zuazo assumes power.

1985   Víctor Paz Estenssoro is elected president by Congress after failing to win a majority of the popular vote.

1986   U.S. military personnel help Bolivian police destroy drug laboratories in the Oriente, where coca leaves are processed into paste.

1989   A civilian presidency completes its full term for the first time since 1964 when Jaime Paz Zamora succeeds Estenssoro as president. The government steps up its measures to crush the Bolivian coca trade, creating the Rural Police Force and announcing plans to build several helicopter bases in the Oriente.

La Paz is a sprawling city that mixes modern structures with old colonial architecture.

1

Bolivia and the World

On the windswept high plateau called the *altiplano*, in western Bolivia, the 20th century seems to have bypassed this South American country entirely. Little has changed here since the rulers of the Inca Empire reigned over the territory more than 400 years ago. The Indians of the region, many of whom are the descendants of the Incas, to a large extent still follow the ways of their ancestors.

They continue to work the neat, stone-rimmed terraces tilled by their forebears and to dress in striped ponchos and brightly colored *winchas* (headbands). They travel the old Inca highway, which at the height of the empire in the 15th century stretched from northern Ecuador to southern Bolivia. Age-old rituals to the earth goddess Pachamama and to Ekeko, the god of prosperity and good fortune, play an important part in their everyday lives.

Yet just east of the altiplano, Bolivia catches up with the 20th century. In La Paz, the country's largest city, the modern world mingles with the ancient. Here, elaborately ornamented 18th-century churches and white-plastered houses built centuries ago by Spanish colonists stand next to geometric skyscrapers and apartment towers.

Outside the cities, the people in the rural communities still dress and work as they have for centuries.

Indian women dressed in colorful skirts and black bowler hats line La Paz's streets, selling everything from potatoes and *quinoa* (a high-protein grain) to good-luck charms and herbal remedies. These market women are said to be barometers of the country's political disposition and are often outspoken critics of the government.

Political instability runs like a dominant thread throughout Bolivia's history. Since it gained independence from Spain in 1825, the country has had 17 constitutions and no fewer than 60 leaders. Thousands of years of Indian civilization, 3 centuries of Spanish domination, and 165 years of independence have given Bolivia a rich and complex history, but they have also created a lingering climate of political and economic disturbances and social injustice.

Until 1952, when a national revolution toppled the powerful and often corrupt ruling class, most Indians (who make up the majority of the population of Bolivia) could not vote or own land. Although Bolivia has some of the world's richest mineral deposits, it is still one of the poorest countries in South America because it lacks the money to explore and develop its mineral wealth. Similarly, the altiplano is extensively farmed, but its soil is not very fertile, and Bolivia must import some of its food. Some communities, faced with poverty, have discovered that they can make more money by growing coca—a shrub that is the source of the illegal drug cocaine—than by growing food to eat or sell. By the late 1980s, Bolivia was producing at least one-third of all the raw coca that made its way into the international cocaine industry.

Bolivia may lack material wealth, but it is abundantly rich in both Indian and Spanish culture and traditions. In many areas, Indian and Catholic religious beliefs have merged to produce a unique faith that recognizes both Christian saints and Indian gods. Ornate churches dating from the colonial era can be found in almost every major city as well as in many small towns; they are a testament to the great wealth produced by the silver mines of Upper Peru, as Bolivia was called under Spanish rule. Many people still speak Quechua and Aymara, the languages of the principal Indian tribes that occupied Bolivia at the time of the Spanish conquest.

The combination of ancient and modern qualities, Indian and Spanish heritages, gives Bolivia a distinctive culture. That the country has survived the ravages of almost constant political, social, and economic strife is a tribute to its proud and resilient people. The Indians maintained their traditions in the face of conquest by the Spanish, and the Spanish colonists in turn succeeded in winning their independence from Spain. Today, as modern Bolivians, they face the challenges of maintaining a stable government, shoring up their weak economy, and controlling the production of and traffic in illegal drugs.

An Aymara man on Lake Titicaca fishes from his boat made from **totora** *reeds, which grow along the edges of the water.*

2

The Rooftop
of the World

Bolivia is a land of geographic extremes. It contains parts of the two dominant land features of the South American continent: the Andes Mountains, which run like a jagged spine from north to south along the western edge of the continent, and the Amazon River basin, which is the enormous sprawling lowland in the northeastern part of the continent that is drained by the thousands of rivers and streams that empty into the Amazon River.

Bolivia is the fifth-largest country in South America. It has a total area of 424,162 square miles (1,111,304 square kilometers). Bolivia is surrounded by Brazil on the north and east, Paraguay on the southeast, Argentina on the south, and Chile and Peru on the west. Bolivia was once almost twice its present size and extended all the way to the Pacific Ocean in the west. In the past 200 years, however, Bolivia has lost territory to all of its neighbor countries and is now landlocked.

The country can be divided into three geographic regions that descend like a trio of steps from west to east. These regions are the Andean Highlands, the Yungas, and the Oriente.

The altiplano, *one of the three main regions of Bolivia, supports most of the country's population.*

The Andean Highlands

The highlands, which dominate the western quarter of Bolivia, are part of the central Andes mountain system. The highlands region consists of two ranges of peaks that hover like mute giants above the altiplano, which lies between them. The western *cordillera*, or range, marks the boundary between Bolivia and Chile. Sparsely populated, with an average elevation of 16,500 feet (5,000 meters), the western cordillera is extremely dry and contains some active volcanoes. The highest point in Bolivia is located here; it is Mount Sajama, and its height is 21,391 feet (6,482 meters) above sea level.

The eastern cordillera, on the other hand, is broken up by fertile valleys and swift-flowing rivers. It contains much of the country's mineral wealth. For most of its course, the eastern cordillera averages 18,000 feet (5,450 meters) in height. Its highest peak is Mount Illimani, which rises to 21,201 feet (6,425 meters) above sea level.

Wedged between the two cordilleras is the high plateau known as the altiplano. This flat, barren land stretches for more than 500 miles (800 kilometers) from southern Peru to northern Argentina, crossing western Bolivia on the way. Almost 150 miles (240 kilometers) across at its greatest width, the altiplano is the largest plateau in the Andes system. Its desolate landscape and somber brown and gray tones give it a moonlike appearance. With an average elevation of 12,000 feet (3,600 meters) above sea level, the altiplano is one of the highest inhabited areas in the world, a distinction that has earned Bolivia the nickname "the rooftop of the world."

Despite its altitude and its lack of fertile farmland, the altiplano is the most populated region of Bolivia. Nearly half the country's people live here. This bleak, stark, yet strangely beautiful land has sustained human life for thousands of years. It was home to three ancient Indian cultures: the Tiahuanaco, the Inca, and the Aymara.

The dry and stony soil of the altiplano supports only a few plants and animals. Clumps of a spiky, strawlike grass, known as *ichu* in Quechua and *paja brava* (savage straw) in Spanish, poke through the parched earth. Highlanders cover their adobe houses with it; llamas, alpacas, and vicuñas, all related to camels and native to the altiplano, feed on its bristly shoots. The twiggy *tola* bush and a native Andean herb called the *yareta* can also withstand the harsh altiplano climate. These plants provide important sources of fuel in a region where trees are scarce. Among the trees that do grow at such high, cold altitudes are the *kishuara*, a native olive tree, and the eucalyptus, which was brought to the highlands from Australia in the mid-19th century.

Along the banks of Lake Titicaca on the northwestern edge of the plateau, thick bunches of the versatile *totora* reeds line the shore. For hundreds of years the Indians have woven these reeds into banana-shaped boats called *balsas*. They also use the reeds as thatch for their houses and as food for their cattle. They spin the plant's fibers into thread for cloth and boil them into soup. The wild *kantuta*, or cornflower, grows on the shores of Lake Titicaca as well and is Bolivia's national emblem.

Llamas and alpacas can still be found on the altiplano and the slopes of the cordilleras, but the vicuña, an endangered species protected by law, is an uncommon sight. The squirrellike chinchilla and its cousin, the vizcacha, also inhabit the altiplano, although their numbers are dwindling. The condor, believed by the Incas to be the messenger of the sun god, still soars among the Andean peaks. Around Lake Titicaca, ducks, geese, plovers, ibis, and gulls abound, and flamingos are found on the banks of Lake Poopó in the central highlands. The rhea, a South American relative of the ostrich, inhabits the southern part of the plateau.

The Yungas and Valles

East of the altiplano, the descending terrain is marked by broad river basins and steep mountain valleys. This area is known as the Yungas, which is an Aymara word that means "warm lands" (the Aymara considered them warm in comparison with the chilly

The vicuña is similar to the alpaca and the llama, but the higher quality of its wool has put the animal in greater demand; so many have been killed that the vicuña has become an endangered species.

Darwin's rhea is a smaller version of the ostrich, but it lives exclusively on the high plains of South America.

altiplano). The Yungas cover approximately 15 percent of Bolivia's total territory and link the high plateau of western Bolivia with the eastern lowlands of the Oriente. They contain several distinct ecological zones, including cool dry plains, fertile semitropical valleys, and hot tropical forests.

The Valles (valleys) are a series of gentle hills in the southern Yungas region. They are the source of most of the food produced in Bolivia. Their rich soil, mild climate, and abundant rainfall give rise to a remarkable variety of plant life. Mahogany, walnut, cedar, laurel, and a host of other trees appear in dense clusters on the slopes and in the valleys at altitudes of 3,000 to 9,000 feet (900 to 2,700 meters). At lower elevations palm trees are common. The quebracho tree also grows here, its exceptionally hard wood providing timber for building materials and fuel as well as a chemical called tannin that is used in tanning hides and making certain

Indian homes in the Oriente reflect the availability of materials in a tropical lowland climate.

medicines. Vanilla, sarsaparilla, and saffron plants, which are made into numerous flavorings and medicines, thrive in the warm, wet climate. Farther east in the Yungas, where the elevations are lower, semitropical and tropical fruits abound. These include bananas, pineapples, avocados, mangoes, and figs.

One of the most significant plants found in the Yungas is the native Andean coca bush. Although the highland Indians have chewed the leaves of this shrub for hundreds of years and have incorporated its use into their culture, today many Bolivians have begun to till new coca fields. The coca leaves are processed into the drug cocaine, which plays a large part in the international drug economy. It is difficult to convince Bolivian peasants to stop growing coca, partly because the leaf is a traditional element of their culture and partly because as a cash crop it brings in more money than would beans or potatoes.

In the humid jungles of the lower Yungas, the jaguar, badger, and piglike peccary are found. Squirrels, opossums, and various types of monkeys are also common. Several varieties of hummingbirds live in the valleys. Many of these creatures, as well as anteaters, tapirs, armadillos, ocelots, and deer, also inhabit the tropical forests and open plains of the Oriente, the third geographic region of Bolivia.

The Oriente

The Oriente, the eastern lowland, is by far the largest of the three regions. It covers about two-thirds of Bolivia's territory, but it contains only one-fourth of the country's population. The Oriente is sometimes referred to as the *llano*, or plain, and indeed it is quite flat. It consists of tropical rain forests in the north and grasslands in the south.

The northern tropical rain forest, or *selva*, is part of the Amazon River basin. Its wide, slow-moving rivers flow northward and eventually empty into the Amazon River in Brazil. The forests are made up of immense evergreen, rubber, and chestnut trees; the thick canopy of their leaves blocks the sunlight and prevents undergrowth. As a result, the interior of the tropical forest has something of the quality of a majestic cathedral, with towering trunks, arching branches, and deeply shaded clearings.

In the central llano, the rain forest gives way to broad, grassy savannas and isolated wooded areas between the waterways. These *pampa*, as the savannas are called, provide ideal grazing land for cattle and are the center of Bolivia's cattle-raising industry. The extreme southeastern tip of the country is a much drier, desertlike area known as the Gran Chaco. It extends into Paraguay and is sprinkled with quebracho and palm trees, scrub brush, and cacti.

Many of the country's major rivers lazily traverse the eastern lowlands. In the north, the mountain-fed Madre de Dios, Beni, and Mamoré rivers converge near the Brazilian border and flow into the

Madeira River, a primary tributary of the Amazon River. Another tributary of the Amazon, the Guaporé River, separates Bolivia from Brazil. And in the south the 1,000-mile-long (1,610-kilometer-long) Pilcomayo River bisects the southern Valles and a portion of the Gran Chaco. The rivers of the Oriente not only provide rich soil for the land surrounding the waterways but also serve as the principal avenues of transport, as few roads penetrate the region. Turtles, alligators, otters, and capybaras (large aquatic rodents sometimes called river hogs) inhabit the waters of the Oriente, as do the flesh-eating piranha fish.

On the altiplano, few waterways of any consequence exist, with the exception of the Desaguadero River. The Desaguadero begins at the southern shore of Lake Titicaca and flows south to Lake Poopó, some 200 miles (320 kilometers) downstream. The two bodies of water it connects are the country's primary lakes.

The Sacred Lake of the Inca and Aymara

On the northern edge of the high plateau are the dazzlingly blue waters of Lake Titicaca, which Bolivia shares with Peru. The largest lake in South America, measuring approximately 138 miles (222 kilometers) long and 70 miles (113 kilometers) wide at its widest point, Lake Titicaca is lined with densely populated settlements and well-tended fields. Its deep waters teem with trout and bass.

According to legend, it was from the shimmering, cobalt blue depths of Lake Titicaca that Viracocha, the creator lord of the Aymara Indians, emerged to call forth the Aymara race. And it was on the Island of Titicaca (now called the Island of the Sun) that the Inca sun god created his children, Manco Capac and Mama Ojllo. According to Inca mythology, these two established the Inca Empire in southern Peru.

Two hundred miles (320 kilometers) south of the sacred lake of the Incas and Aymaras lies shallow, salty Lake Poopó. Twenty miles (32 kilometers) wide and 56 miles (90 kilometers) long, Lake Poopó frequently spills its briny waters into the surrounding region, nourishing the huge salt flats southwest of the lake. Here the characteristically dry altiplano becomes even drier and the landscape more barren. The average yearly rainfall is less than 5 inches (127 millimeters).

Elsewhere on the altiplano more rain falls, although the highlands in general receive less precipitation than the rest of the country. Rainfall around Lake Titicaca averages 28 inches (711 millimeters) annually; near La Paz the average decreases to 23 inches (584 millimeters). In the Yungas, where heavy mists often shroud the mountains, the average yearly rainfall ranges from 50 to 192 inches (1,270 to 4,877 millimeters) on the northern slopes and from 18 to 35 inches (457 to 889 millimeters) in the southern Valles. The heaviest precipitation occurs in the rain forest of the northern Oriente, where the rivers frequently overflow, forcing the few inhabitants to seek refuge on high land. Farther south, around Santa Cruz, rainfall averages 30 to 50 inches (762 to 1,270 millimeters) annually.

The rainy season in Bolivia occurs between December and late March; this is summer in the Southern Hemisphere. Daytime temperatures during the summer can reach as high as 80 degrees Fahrenheit (26 degrees Celsius) on the altiplano, although cooler temperatures are the rule there. Frost frequently cloaks the high plateau regardless of the season, and razor-sharp winds often make the region seem even colder than it is. Temperatures in the Yungas range from 72 degrees Fahrenheit (22 degrees Celsius) in January to 52 degrees Fahrenheit (11 degrees Celsius) in July. Temperatures in the Oriente average around 80 degrees Fahrenheit (26 degrees Celsius) year-round.

Remnants of the 3,000-year-old Tiahuanaco ruins include 13-foot monoliths such as this one, carved from lava.

3

Indian Empires and Spanish Rule

Long before Christopher Columbus dropped anchor in the Western Hemisphere, Indian civilizations had already reached high levels of development in the Americas. In the Bolivian highlands, just a few miles south of Lake Titicaca, lie the ruins of the ancient city of Tiahuanaco, the first great central Andean civilization. Archaeologists have unearthed the foundations of various buildings and several huge stone monuments, some weighing as much as 100 tons (111 metric tons), but scholars still know little about the city or the culture that created it.

The Tiahuanaco culture is believed to have appeared on the altiplano about 100 B.C. and to have reached its peak at about A.D. 900. It dominated the central Andean highlands—and possibly extended even farther—from 600 to 1000. Traces of the Tiahuanaco civilization have surfaced in Colombia, Argentina, and Chile and along the coast of Peru.

The elaborately chiseled figures and extraordinary stonework of these ruins suggest that Tiahuanaco was one of the most complex and advanced Indian cultures of its time. Two structures, the Gate of the Sun and the Kalasasaya in Tiahuanaco, are made from enormous stone blocks that were quarried more than 150 miles (240 kilometers) away. The central feature of the Gate of the Sun, which was carved from a solitary slab of rock weighing more than 10 tons (11 metric tons), is the figure of the sun god above the doorway. Spokes, or rays, emanate from its rectangular head, and tears in the shapes of condors' and snakes' heads trail across its timeworn cheeks. Each hand clasps a chiseled staff topped with the head of an animal.

The Gate of the Sun is located on the Kalasasaya, a rectangular platform consisting of a courtyard and living areas thought to have been occupied by the city's priests. The stones that form the base of this structure are pieced together with great precision, which indicates a level of technology far more advanced than most other South American Indian cultures of this period. Several gargantuan statues with humanlike features have been excavated as well. According to one story told by the Aymara Indians, who are believed to be the descendants of the people of Tiahuanaco, these figures were the first human beings created by Viracocha, their creator lord. But these giant men and women somehow incurred the anger of their creator and were turned to stone as punishment, thereafter standing as silent sentinels over the windswept heights of Tiahuanaco.

The Rise of the Aymara Civilization

After the collapse of the Tiahuanaco culture around A.D. 1200, the Indians of the region formed the Aymara culture, which consisted of a number of small, independent, loosely allied states. Each state was divided into two parts, and each of these parts had a separate government that was headed by a hereditary ruler. In addition to belonging to a state, every person was a member of an *ayllu*, a community of people related to each other. According to Aymara belief, the original members of each ayllu were spawned from a natural landmark located near the ayllu's community. Like the states, ayllus were divided into two halves, an upper and a lower group. The rulers and members of the nobility belonged to the upper half, and the commoners belonged to the lower half.

These long-ago ancestors of the contemporary Aymara raised potatoes and quinoa on the terraced hillsides once worked by the people of Tiahuanaco. Land belonged to the entire ayllu rather than to individuals, and the members tilled the earth communally. They tended large herds of llamas and alpacas, which provided them with meat, dung for fuel, and wool for clothing. Each state and ayllu maintained colonies in the mountain valleys east of the altiplano and along the Pacific coast to the west; the colonies cultivated the products of these regions. Although the Aymara did not use money, a complex network of trade developed among the regions. The products of the highlands were exchanged for fish and salt from the coast and for corn, coca, and fruits from the eastern valleys.

Numerous Puquina-speaking tribes, such as the Uru and the Chipaya, lived among the Aymaras. They often worked as laborers for the Aymara. According to Uru oral tradition, the Uru frequently served as unwilling human sacrifices in Aymara rituals. The Chipaya escaped much of the misery that was thrust upon the Uru. They scratched a meager living from the parched earth of the southern altiplano and raised llamas to supplement their scanty agricultural output.

A number of other Indian groups lived in the Oriente. Most of them were roving hunter-gatherers who did not establish permanent villages. Various Amazonian tribes that spoke the Arawakan language of northern South America and the Caribbean lived in Bolivia's northern rain forests. Tribes from the Guaraní culture that was native to the Atlantic coast migrated from what is now Paraguay and settled on Bolivia's southern plain.

Despite the daunting barrier of the eastern cordillera that separates the altiplano from the Oriente, the Indians of the two regions periodically clashed in disputes over territory. The lowland Indians acquired a reputation as fierce and unconquerable opponents. As a result, the tribes of the Oriente were spared the fate suffered by the Aymara in the 15th century, when a new and aggressive Indian culture entered the altiplano from the north. These newcomers were the Quechua Indians of southern Peru. They overcame the Aymara and incorporated their lands into the Quechua empire.

The Empire of the Sun

The Quechua, or Inca as they are more widely known, founded their empire around A.D. 1100. At its peak in the early 16th century, this empire encompassed about 380,000 square miles (995,600 square kilometers) and embraced parts of present-day Ecuador, Peru, Bolivia, Chile, and Argentina.

As with the Aymara, the ayllu formed the basis of the Inca political and economic system. The Inca also developed one of the most elaborate social structures in all of pre-Columbian America, with a complex hierarchy of workers, bosses, foremen, headmen, district governors, and governors leading up to the emperor at the top of the social pyramid. Many of the governors and district governors were relatives of the Inca emperor.

According to Inca mythology, the emperor was a descendant of the sun and was therefore a god. He looked after his subjects by protecting them against attack and by designing such projects as roads and irrigation canals. In return, the people paid taxes in the form of crops and labor. Each ayllu member worked a portion of the ayllu's lands on behalf of the emperor and the sun god, setting these crops aside for official use. Obligatory labor was known as the *mita*. Individuals could be drafted to help build roads and bridges, to work in the gold and silver mines, to serve in the Inca army, or to spin wool and weave articles of clothing. If the nature of the work required a person to leave his community for a while, the members of the ayllu took over the cultivation of his lands during his absence.

The Spanish Conquest

The golden era of Inca rule ended in 1532, when a group of Spanish conquistadores led by Francisco Pizarro landed at Tumbes, on the northern coast of what is now Peru. The timing of his arrival was lucky for the Spanish: A five-year war between the emperor Atahuallpa and his brother had significantly weakened the empire. Pizarro and his Spanish soldiers attacked the Inca, killing thousands and capturing Atahuallpa.

The imprisoned ruler promised to fill the spacious room in which he was held with gold and silver in exchange for his freedom. Soon, riches from all four quarters of the empire poured into Cajamarca, where he was held, but the Spanish killed him anyway in July 1533. Without a central ruler to unify the people, Inca society was immobilized. In less than a year Pizarro had taken control of one of the most powerful Indian empires in South America. His half brother

Inca filled a room with silver objects to ransom their emperor Atahuallpa. In 1533, the Spanish killed him anyway, and the Inca Empire toppled.

The Inca were known for their intricate silver ornaments, but most were destroyed by the Spanish. This late-15th-century silver alpaca is one of the few Inca ornaments to survive.

Hernando Pizarro completed the conquest of the southern branch of the empire—in what is now Bolivia—in 1538.

The Mountain of Silver

That same year, as the Spanish began to explore the Bolivian altiplano, they also established mining settlements at Chuquisaca (now called Sucre) and Porco. In 1545, they found the riches for which they had launched their war of conquest. An Indian in the employ of a Spanish captain discovered the Cerro Rico, or Rich Mountain, which was almost solid silver.

The Inca had known about the wealth that lay hidden in this cone-shaped hill, but they refused to exploit its vast lodes of silver. According to legend, in the 15th century the Inca emperor Huayna Capac had come upon the mountain and commanded his subjects to begin excavating it. As they did, a horrible voice ordered them to cease their digging because the riches the hill contained were destined for others. The terrified Indians fled from the mountain screaming, "The mountain is falling down!"

Less than a hundred years later, the Spanish founded a mining town called Potosí at the base of the hill. Thousands of Spanish subjects eager to make a quick fortune began to pour into the streets of the crude frontier settlement. Potosí soon became one of the largest cities in the New World, where the brutal exploitation of Indian labor was the foundation for extraordinary wealth and opulence. Thousands of Indians from the surrounding regions were forced to work in the mines under deplorable and dangerous conditions. The Spanish made the Indian workers stay in the mines six days a week to eliminate the time spent changing shifts. The workers ate and slept in a world of darkness, the flame of their candles the only light that illuminated their lives. On Sundays, when the miners were allowed to emerge from their hot, damp underworld, the temperatures on the altiplano frequently hovered near the freezing mark. Until the 1550s the Indians were not paid for their services, but even after new laws required them to be paid, the amount they received was so small that it barely kept them alive. It has been said that the silver mined from the Cerro Rico could have produced a bridge one yard (one meter) wide between Potosí and Spain. It has also been said that a second bridge could have been made from the bones of the Indian laborers who died extracting the precious metal from the bowels of the mountain.

The rapid growth of Potosí led to the establishment of other important centers in Upper Peru, as Bolivia was called by the Spanish. In 1548, they founded the city of La Paz as a way station for the llama trains that carted silver, silks, and a variety of other goods between Potosí and Lima, Peru. Potosí's growing population required more food, so the Spanish established the town of Villa de Oropeza (now Cochabamba) in a fertile eastern valley to help supply Potosí's agricultural needs. Three years later they built another agricultural center, Tarija, in the southern Valles. And in 1606, the city of Oruro was established after silver was discovered nearby.

The Conquered and the Conquerors

By the beginning of the 17th century, Peru was a thriving Spanish colony, but its prosperity was utterly dependent upon widespread exploitation of the Indians. In addition to working in the mines, Indian men labored in the fields and textile factories of their conquerors. As the Spanish settled the lands of the altiplano and eastern valleys, they divided portions of the former Inca territory into *encomiendas*, or grants. Huge tracts of land and all the Indian communities that they contained were placed under the control of *encomenderos*, or grant holders, who in theory at least were responsible for teaching the Indians the tenets of Roman Catholicism as well as introducing them to the ways of Spanish society. The encomenderos set taxes and collected them from the Indians. As a result, many encomenderos grew quite rich, but the majority of the Indian population seldom rose above poverty.

Not all Spaniards, however, approved of this exploitation. Priests and missionaries in particular protested the mistreatment of the Indians. In 1542, at their urging, King Charles I of Spain issued a code of laws that abolished the encomienda system. Although the New Laws, as they were known, were never strictly enforced and some encomiendas continued to function, many encomiendas did disappear. But they were soon replaced by a similar system, based on the *hacienda*, or large estate, that started in the arable valleys of the Yungas and around Lake Titicaca.

Only the Jesuits, members of a Roman Catholic religious order noted for its intellectual achievements, treated the Indians fairly. While attempting to convert the Indians to the Roman Catholic

This is Potosí as it looks today. At the height of its prosperity in 1650, Potosí had a population of 160,000. Although it is a leading industrial center producing iron and steel and mining tin, lead, and copper, the city's population is roughly 103,000.

faith, the Jesuits helped the Indians prosper as farmers by introducing them to cattle breeding as well as to such new crops as wheat and oranges.

The arrival of the Spanish signaled not only the fall of the Inca Empire but also the rapid decline of the Indian population. The mines claimed as many as 80 percent of all workers; other Indians fell victim to new diseases introduced by the Spaniards, such as smallpox and measles. The reduction of the native population throughout South America was so severe that by the beginning of the 19th century, the Indians numbered less than half of what they had numbered before the Spanish conquest (some sources say even fewer).

The hacienda is a lasting example of the country's Spanish influence.

The Decline of Colonial Rule

Around the middle of the 17th century, the treasures of the Cerro Rico and the mines at Oruro began to give out. The decline of Upper Peru's most important industry plunged the region into a century-long depression, the effects of which were felt in every part of the colony. The mining centers that had once attracted thousands of fortune seekers now emptied out. By 1750, more than half of the inhabitants of Potosí and Oruro had moved on to other places. The demand for food thus decreased, and many haciendas in the Yungas became idle. The economic slowdown brought about by the depression somewhat relieved the pressures on the Indians, and between 1650 and 1750 the Indian population increased.

By the mid-18th century, the period of Spanish colonial rule in Upper Peru was nearing its end. Uprisings and revolts had rocked the Andean highlands from the time the first conquistadores had set foot on Peruvian soil. These conflicts involved fighting between rival Spanish factions and individuals as well as sporadic Indian rebellions. The Spanish always quelled the rebellions before they became serious. But in 1780, stretched to the limit by mistreatment at the hands of the corrupt and abusive colonial officials, the Indians rose up in revolt. Led by Tupac Amarú, a highly educated Indian who claimed to be descended from the last Inca ruler, the rebels attempted to expel the Spaniards from the Andes and restore Inca rule. Bands of Indians terrorized the countryside, attacking villages, destroying property, and killing many Spanish officials. For more than 100 days, the rebel Indians laid siege to La Paz. Tupac Amarú was captured and executed in May 1781, but the struggle continued under other leaders for two more years until the Spanish finally stamped out the uprising.

At the same time, the Spanish themselves—descendants of the original colonists, many of whom had intermarried with Indians, as well as new colonists from Europe—were growing increasingly dissatisfied with Spain's rule. They wanted to control the government and tax revenues of Upper Peru themselves.

Almost 30 years after the Indian rebellion was put down, the simmering political discontent of 3 centuries finally came to a head. In 1809, white and mestizo (mixed white and Indian) colonists in Chuquisaca, Cochabamba, Oruro, and Potosí rebelled against the Spanish authorities and declared their independence. But the viceroy of Lima, who was the senior representative of Spain in the western part of South America, quickly dispatched a force of 5,000 soldiers to crush the revolts. The Spanish army easily defeated the rebels, who numbered only about 1,000. In January 1810, the rebel leader Pedro Domingo Murillo went to his execution saying, "No one will extinguish the spark I leave behind me." The first call for Bolivian independence had been sounded.

Simón Bolívar freed Peru, Venezuela, Colombia, and Ecuador as well as Bolivia from Spanish rule.

4

The Republic of Bolivia

For 16 years following the 1809 rebellion, rebel forces led by José Francisco de San Martín and Simón Bolívar struggled to wrench the American colonies free from Spanish domination. By 1821, San Martín's army had reached Lima, and the enthusiastic Peruvians proclaimed their independence. But the imperial army still occupied the highlands of Upper Peru, and it would be another four years before Bolívar's forces defeated the Spanish there.

By 1822, Bolívar had liberated Venezuela, Colombia, and Ecuador from Spanish rule. He then marched on Peru, where, with his lieutenant, Antonio José de Sucre, he proceeded to dislodge the last of the Spanish supporters from their stronghold on the altiplano. On August 6, 1824, he squared off with the Spanish forces at the battle of Junín in the central Peruvian highlands, and four months later Sucre defeated the remaining royalist holdouts at Ayacucho. In February 1825, the victorious Sucre entered La Paz.

The First Years of Independence
On August 6, 1825, an assembly of representatives of Upper Peru declared the region an independent republic, to be named after Bolívar. Bolívar himself wrote the new nation's constitution, which

41

stipulated that only citizens who could read and write were allowed to vote. As most of the population was illiterate, this provision automatically excluded the majority of Bolivians from choosing their leaders, and it would cause political problems throughout the country's future.

In 1826, Bolivia's select group of voters elected Antonio José de Sucre as the nation's first president, and the war hero began to carry out reforms that Bolívar had set in motion. But reform proved to be difficult in an economically devastated country with a population that was divided into mutually hostile groups: the Spanish, mestizos, and Indians. Sucre's efforts did not bring about reform fast enough, and the Bolivian army grew disenchanted with its president. After a failed assassination attempt, Sucre resigned from office in 1828 and died in exile two years later.

Sucre was replaced by General Andrés Santa Cruz, another veteran of the wars of independence. A mestizo born in La Paz, Santa Cruz had served in the Spanish army but had joined forces with the patriot cause in 1821. Eight years after he took office, Santa Cruz overthrew the president of Peru and created the Peru-Bolivian Confederation with himself as its "protector," or leader. News of the alliance enormously displeased the leaders of Chile and Argentina, who feared it would tip the scale of South American power in favor of the new confederation. Both countries sent soldiers to topple Santa Cruz, and he was eventually ousted in 1839. His defeat established a pattern of military overthrow that would plague Bolivian politics for the next 150 years.

Indian Life in the New Republic

Although Bolívar had eliminated forced labor after the revolution, little had really changed for the Indians of Bolivia. American-born Bolivians of Spanish descent and high-ranking mestizos had quickly assumed the places of power previously held by their Spanish predecessors. Many Indians still toiled on the lands of the elite, still

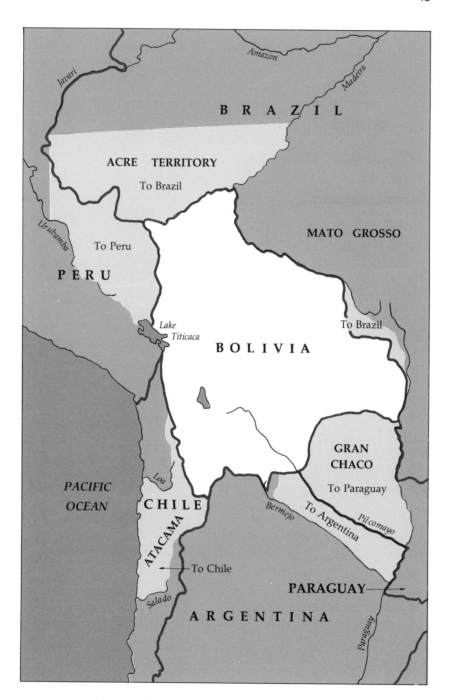

labored long hours for the hacienda owners, and still owned none of their own land. With most mines in ruins and no funds to restore them, the Indians were spared the atrocities of mining, but they were also deprived of the income that mining had brought.

A few of the nation's early leaders, such as Manuel Isidoro Belzú (president, 1848–55), tried to improve the condition of the Indians and mestizos. A mestizo himself, Belzú called for programs to educate the Indian peasants and encouraged their participation in the government of the country. However, the elite ruling class opposed him, and he resigned in 1855 after a series of uprisings among the army and the lower classes.

Belzú returned in 1865 to topple the presidency of Mariano Melgarejo, who had taken office a year earlier by means of a military coup d'état. As the deposed Melgarejo was about to abdicate his short-lived office, he embraced Belzú and fatally shot him. Melgarejo then walked out onto the balcony of the presidential palace, announced that Belzú was dead, and reclaimed the presidency. The six years of rule that followed proved to be among the blackest in Bolivian history. A brutal dictator, Melgarejo often used force to silence his opponents.

In 1866, he declared that all ayllu lands farmed by the Indians would be parceled up and sold. Any Indian who did not pay the required sum within 60 days would lose title to the land. The Indian could, however, rent the land from the state if no one purchased it at auction. As most Indians were living in dire poverty, the majority of them could not afford to buy land, and the bulk of their property went to wealthy whites and mestizos.

War and Politics

Bolivia still needed money, and in 1878 the government put a heavy tax on the minerals called nitrates that were exported from its Pacific coast region to Chile and Europe, where their principal use was in the manufacture of fertilizer. Over the years, however, Chileans had slowly penetrated this part of Bolivia until it had become more Chilean than Bolivian. Controversy over the new tax gave Chile the excuse it had been seeking to claim the region as its own. In February 1879, Chilean troops landed at the port of Antofagasta, and in a short time all major ports in the disputed region were in Chilean hands. In April, Bolivia and its ally Peru declared war on Chile, but Bolivia was poorly prepared for war. By the end of the year, the Bolivians were defeated. Bolivia forfeited all its coastal territory to Chile and has been landlocked ever since.

The military government lost power after its defeat in the War of the Pacific, but a new force emerged in Bolivia: political parties. Mine owners and landowners of the altiplano formed the Liberal and Conservative parties in the 1880s. At this time, the country entered a period of relative political and economic stability.

The Rule of the Rosca

This stability came from the emergence of an aristocracy, which had been created by a boom in silver mining in the 1870s and tin mining in the early 20th century. The tin baron Simón Patiño, his partner Mauricio Hochschild, and the silver-mining Aramago family controlled the bulk of Bolivia's mining industry and much of the Bolivian government as well. Patiño in particular became one of the wealthiest men in the world as a result of the tin boom. In the early 20th century, this mining aristocracy became known as the *rosca*, and it began to prop up Bolivia's political parties the way the army had supported military dictators in the 19th century.

The nation's leaders were the rosca's puppets, and they acted in the interests of the mine owners and hacienda owners. Many of the public works projects undertaken during the early 20th century, such as the construction of railroads and the installation of electricity, were prompted by the rosca and benefited the entire country. Still, only about 5 percent of the population could vote, and Indians, who made up 80 percent of the population, were completely isolated from participation in the government. The failure of Bolivia's aristocracy and its government to address these social and economic concerns became evident in the following years, during the Chaco War.

The Chaco War

For years Bolivia and Paraguay had squabbled over the ownership of portions of the Gran Chaco region in southern Bolivia because both countries believed that this desert wasteland might be hiding valuable oil fields. Minor skirmishes erupted sporadically between their armies. The tension mounted, until Bolivian president Daniel

The Chaco War put Indians, mestizos, cholos, and blancos side by side in combat; this mixing of cultures paved the way for a philosophy of reform in subsequent governments.

Salamanca used one of the skirmishes as an opportunity to bolster his waning popularity and launched an all-out attack. But, as had happened with the War of the Pacific, the Bolivian military was ill prepared for war. Within three months the Paraguayan army had advanced into Bolivia.

With these defeats and the mounting number of Bolivian casualties, public opinion began to shift against the government. By the middle of 1933, the incompetence of Bolivia's military leaders had killed thousands in the Chaco, and thousands more perished from malnutrition and illness on the sweltering southern plains. Those who suffered most were the Indians and the *cholos* (mestizos of the lower classes), as these groups formed the majority of the troops.

The war dragged on for another year and a half, with the Paraguayan forces moving farther and farther into Bolivian territory. Then, in the first months of 1935, the tide began to turn. The Bolivian army routed the Paraguayans from Tarija and Santa Cruz. By May 1935, both sides had had enough of war, and they agreed to meet in Buenos Aires, Argentina, to discuss an end to the fighting. On June 14, they signed a formal peace treaty, and the Chaco War was over. Bolivia had lost 100,000 square miles (260,000 square kilometers) of its Chaco territory.

The Chaco War brought about enormous political and social changes in Bolivia. It completely discredited the wealthy ruling class that had supported the government, and it unleashed the military's long-suppressed influence on politics. In 1934, the army forced President Salamanca to resign, sparking a complicated and often violent series of military coups that lasted until the early 1980s.

The most important figure from this period is Colonel Germán Busch, a Chaco War hero who seized power in 1937 and declared himself dictator. He is known chiefly for establishing labor reforms during his two-year reign. Previous governments had initiated social reforms by taking control of the United States–owned Standard Oil Company (which had been suspected of playing a key role in starting the Chaco War) and by encouraging organized labor. Busch established the first labor codes, which abolished the indentured farming system under which the peasant Indian population had suffered, and he regulated the mining industry. He became a kind of national martyr-hero after committing suicide in 1939.

The 1940s saw the emergence of a number of new left-wing and right-wing parties, formed by the nation's professional people, students, and intellectuals, who felt that the Chaco War had been a disgrace. The draft had introduced some young white soldiers to Indian and cholo soldiers, and the educated youth of Bolivia began to better understand their country's cultural divisions. Although each of the new political parties had a distinct point of view, each called for radical change within the government.

The Creation of the MNR

The most popular of these new parties was a group founded by Víctor Paz Estenssoro, called the Movimiento Nacionalista

Víctor Paz Estenssoro was an active political figure in Bolivia's history. He founded the MNR (Movimiento Nacionalista Revolucionario) and served as the country's president twice, from 1952 to 1964 and from 1985 to 1989.

Revolucionario (National Revolutionary Movement, or MNR). It had gained its popularity among the miners in 1942 when it exposed a massacre of unarmed workers and their families by the government during a strike in Oruro.

The MNR was a nationalist party and as such was not necessarily aligned with either leftist or rightist politics. But when pressure from the United States during World War II (1939–45) forced Bolivia to declare war on Germany in 1942, the MNR, believing Bolivia should not involve itself in international conflicts, joined with a pro-Hitler military faction. Under the leadership of Major Gualberto Villarroel, it staged a coup in 1943 and took control of the government.

Despite his fascist alliance, Villarroel started a number of labor reforms, reaching out to the working-class segment of the population and encouraging the nation's tin miners to organize a union. He sought ways to help the Indian population; in May 1945, he convened the country's first national Indian Congress, meeting with more than 1,000 Indian leaders. One of the major resolutions to come out of this convention was the promise to build schools in the Indian communities.

Nevertheless, Villarroel used strong-arm tactics to keep himself in power—tactics such as having his detractors assassinated. Friction within his administration led to his downfall. In July 1946, he and several of his aides were dragged from the presidential palace by a La Paz mob, and he was lynched from a nearby lamppost. With time, however, Villarroel would be remembered as a hero, and the lamppost from which he was hanged would become the unofficial symbol of the Bolivian national revolution.

An Aymara woman makes her way through downtown La Paz after a riot in which students threw cobblestones at the police.

5

Revolution and Reform

Following Gualberto Villarroel's death, Bolivia once again found itself in the hands of a conservative government run by the rosca. But the country had witnessed enormous social and economic changes in the years following the Chaco War. Although the new government tried to reverse the recent gains, it was impossible to return to prewar practices. Popular dissatisfaction with the new regime was fanned by the MNR, which in the years right after Villarroel's death had been banned from participating in the government (some MNR leaders, Víctor Paz Estenssoro in particular, had been exiled). This did not prevent the MNR from continuing to press for reforms, however. Between 1946 and 1951, the party's support increased so much that in the May 1951 presidential elections the MNR won a majority of the votes. But the outgoing regime instead handed the presidency over to the army, which voided the results of the election.

Social and economic troubles, including low tin prices, serious inflation, and the continuing oppression of laborers, spurred the MNR to lead a revolt. On April 9, 1952, with the help of Indian peasants, miners, and some civilian and military groups, Estenssoro led a siege of La Paz and several other cities. After three days of heavy fighting, the Bolivian army buckled, and the MNR was victorious. This became known as the revolution of 1952.

Effects of the National Revolution

The national revolution brought about profound changes within the country. The MNR provided the most stable government in the country's history and allowed such things as a free press to exist. Víctor Paz Estenssoro, now president, virtually eliminated the threat of military overthrow by drastically reducing the size of the army and creating a civilian militia to take its place. He extended voting privileges to all adults, regardless of whether they could read or write. For the first time in Bolivia's history, the majority of the population would have a say in how the government was run.

A number of other reforms helped improve the lives of Indians and miners. Estenssoro established the Ministry of Peasant Affairs to address the concerns of the Indians and to carry out programs on their behalf. Because most of the rural Indian communities did not have even the most basic educational and health care facilities, the ministry strove to establish primary schools and health clinics throughout the countryside. So eager were the Indians to receive these services that they often volunteered to construct the buildings that housed the facilities.

Soon after the April uprising the mine workers established the Central Obrera Boliviana (COB), a national labor federation. One of its first actions was to urge the government to take control of the three major mining companies. In October 1952, the Estenssoro administration acted on this advice, nationalizing the firms and turning them over to the newly organized and state-run Corporación Minera de Bolivia (Bolivian Mining Corporation), or COMIBOL.

Indians played an important role, through their newly created unions, in the drafting of a far-reaching piece of legislation called the Agrarian Reform Law. This law distributed to the Indian peasant farmers the majority of the land that belonged to the wealthy hacienda owners. Finally, the Indians were the undisputed owners of their own land.

Economic reforms came about as well. The MNR developed the country's petroleum industry, investing heavily in equipment for the state-run oil company. The government expanded the network of roadways that connected the outlying Indian communities by building a highway between Cochabamba and Santa Cruz. This ready access to and from Santa Cruz helped spur a period of great growth in the Oriente, a region that traditionally had been the most underpopulated and undeveloped area of Bolivia.

Despite the government's ambitious efforts, a decline in the tin industry and uncontrollable inflation continued to plague Bolivia throughout the 1950s and early 1960s. Gradually, the military began to recover much of its power. René Barrientos Ortuño, an air force general, held the vice-president's seat. Finally, in 1964, after 12 relatively peaceful years of participatory democracy, a military coup once again overthrew the government. Ortuño forced Estenssoro into exile and took control.

Land reform came about as a result of the revolution of 1952, creating a new class of campesinos *from the previously dispossessed Indian populations.*

Military Rule Again

President Ortuño, whose mother was Indian, grew up speaking Quechua and was immensely popular among the peasant population. Backed by foreign aid from the United States, he helped some Indian communities obtain modern agricultural equipment and encouraged them to adopt more productive methods of farming. He also worked diligently to increase the number of schools in Bolivia and to ensure that even the remotest Indian communities had access to educational facilities.

Ortuño's good relations with the peasant farmers did not extend to the working class, however. Extremely wary of the power held by the labor unions, he canceled the workers' right to elect union officials. In addition, he suppressed all strike activity, often by force.

The workers were not the only dissenters the president had to contend with. In 1966, the Argentinean-born Communist revolutionary Ernesto "Che" Guevara established a training camp in the dense jungles of the Oriente, evidently intended as much to serve as a base for his operations in Argentina and Brazil as to carry out a Communist revolution in Bolivia. The United States, deeply concerned about revolutionary activity in Latin America, sent a contingent of soldiers to help the Bolivian army flush the Communist rebels out of their hiding place. By October 1967, Guevara had been captured and killed. Less than two years later, Ortuño himself was killed in a helicopter accident while touring the Bolivian countryside.

The next decade saw a string of military leaders who for the most part ruled for short and stormy tenures. These leaders often sought to silence opposition voices. They banned political parties and labor unions and once closed the universities. Those who disagreed with the regime in power were often exiled or killed. Nevertheless, most Bolivians continued to oppose military rule, and in the late 1970s the government came under increasing pressure from the people to hold free elections. In 1978, 1979, and 1980, elections were

Ernesto "Che" Guevara was a leader in Cuba's Communist revolution; he was killed in Bolivia while trying to organize the workers. Considered a threat by the government, he remains a hero to many Bolivians.

held—only to be annulled (declared void) by the military. During this period, in 1979, Lidia Gueiler became Bolivia's first woman president and the first woman to head any South American government. Her reign, like most of her predecessors', was short lived. A series of strikes and demonstrations by miners and other workers finally convinced the military to return to civilian rule in October 1982. Hernán Siles Zuazo, who had received the most votes in the 1980 presidential election, assumed office.

Return to Civilian Rule

In 1985, Bolivia again held free elections. No candidate received a majority of the votes, so the decision fell to the National Congress, which chose the longtime leader of the MNR, Víctor Paz Estenssoro, who had returned from exile.

When Estenssoro took office, the Bolivian economy was in chaos, and the inflation rate was the highest in the world. In an attempt to revitalize the economy, Estenssoro encouraged the development of new industries so that Bolivia would no longer have to rely solely on mining, its traditional source of national income. By the time he

Workers gather in a La Paz square to hear a speech on the country's debt crisis in 1979. The workers' unions in Bolivia hold much political power.

left office in 1989, inflation had been brought under control and the economy stabilized. Civilian rule has continued under his successor, Jaime Paz Zamora, who had served as vice-president during Zuazo's administration.

Structure of the Government

Bolivia's current constitution is much like that of the United States. It divides the government into three branches of equal power: executive, legislative, and judicial. The executive branch is made up of the president, the vice-president, and the cabinet. The president, who heads the executive branch, is elected by popular vote for a period of four years and may not serve two consecutive terms in office. He or she selects the heads of the various government agencies that are represented on the president's cabinet. The vice-president is elected jointly with the president and serves as the presiding officer of the Senate.

The legislative branch of the government is made up of two houses, which together form the National Congress. The Senate is composed of 27 members, 3 from each of the 9 departments, or districts, into which the country is divided. In the 157-member Chamber of Deputies, on the other hand, the number of deputies from each department is determined by the population of the department: The more populated departments, such as the Department of La Paz, elect more deputies than the less-populated ones, such as the Department of Beni. Congressmen from both houses are elected by popular vote, with senators serving six-year terms and deputies serving four-year terms.

The third branch of the government, the judicial, encompasses the Supreme Court and the lower district and local courts. Unlike the executive and legislative branches, which are based in the administrative capital of La Paz, the judicial branch is based in Sucre, the constitutional capital of Bolivia. Thirteen justices sit on Bolivia's Supreme Court. Congress chooses these court justices with a two-thirds majority vote. Each justice serves for a period of 10 years.

The nine departments of Bolivia are La Paz, Oruro, Potosí, Tarija, Chuquisaca, Cochabamba, Santa Cruz, Beni, and Pando. They are headed by officials appointed by the president, but the national government controls much of what these officials do. Thus, even though the cities and towns are administered by mayors and councils elected by popular vote, the local and departmental governments in reality have very little authority.

Over the past two centuries the economic and social development of Bolivia has been hampered by unstable and often tyrannical governments. Yet despite its stormy history Bolivia is slowly emerging as a democratic, economically secure nation. Though many Bolivians are still poor and live in less than ideal conditions, the revolution of 1952 was a giant leap forward in righting the injustices that have existed in Bolivia for hundreds of years. It is a promising sign that all of the governments since 1952, both civilian and military, have been committed to continuing the reforms begun by the revolution. The country seems to be achieving its primary goal, a stable government. With the inauguration of Jaime Paz Zamora in August 1989, Bolivia completed its first full term of civilian rule and peaceful transfer of power in more than 20 years.

A knitted hat called the lluchu *identifies the altiplano Indian.*

6

People and
Social Services

In a land where one can travel from snow-covered mountains to steamy jungles in a matter of hours, the Bolivian people are as diverse and distinct as the country's changing terrain.

More than half of Bolivia's nearly 7 million people are Indian, although they belong to at least 5 different peoples, each of which has its own customs and style of dress. The largest of these Indian groups are the Quechua, who make up 30 percent of the country's population, and the Aymara, who account for another 25 percent. Mestizos, or Bolivians of mixed Indian and European ancestry, make up 30 percent of the population, and whites of European descent constitute about 14 percent. Less than one percent consists of non-European immigrants; most of them are Asians who emigrated to the Bolivian lowlands in the mid-20th century, and a few are Arabs.

The Indian Population

The largest Indian group within Bolivia, the Quechua, live mostly on the southern altiplano and in the eastern valleys. Most are rural farmers, although some are employed in the mines. They speak the Quechua language, which was the language of the Inca emperors.

The Aymara are concentrated on the northern altiplano in the departments of La Paz and Oruro. Like the Quechua, they are primarily rural farmers who raise crops for their own consumption, rarely selling their produce to outsiders. Their lives are centered on the land and the extended family, and they continue to remain isolated from mainstream Bolivian society, conversing in the Aymara language (although some speak Spanish as well); many of them continue to practice age-old traditional rituals directed at the numerous gods of the Aymara religion.

Language and religion are not the only things that set the Indians apart from their mestizo compatriots. Often an Indian does not even have to speak to reveal his or her heritage, because the style of dress says it all. In the countryside around Sucre, which is predominantly Quechua territory, women wear long black dresses and red or wine-colored shawls bordered with yellow, orange, red, and green. Around La Paz, the Aymara women wear white blouses and *polleras* (full, gathered skirts) in shades of red and blue. During fiestas, they often wear three or four of these skirts at once, and the skirts swirl in great billows of color as they pirouette to music. Over their blouses Aymara women generally wear a short bolero jacket or a knitted cardigan sweater as well as a fringed shawl.

Often the fastest way to tell where a woman is from is to look at her hat. There are about as many different hat styles in Bolivia as there are Indian peoples. Quechua women generally wear tall stovepipe hats that vary in color and fabric from one region to the next. In La Paz and on the northern altiplano, the black bowler hats favored by women bob along the winding streets, their upturned brims set at jaunty angles.

Men's clothing also varies between regions and cultures. A man in or near La Paz is likely to wear baggy wool pants, a shirt, and a loose-fitting suit jacket, sometimes topped off with a long rectangular poncho. Some also wear a pointed hand-knit hat known as a *lluchu* or *chullo*, and sometimes they place a manufactured European-style hat over this. In the valleys southeast of Sucre, Quechua men still wear ponchos fashioned to resemble the breast-plates of the Spanish conquistadores who invaded the region in the 16th century. Their close-fitting, helmetlike hats of black suede also reflect the conquistador influence although the colorful embroidery and sequined trim around the brim are unmistakably Indian touches.

Though the Quechua and Aymara are the principal Indian peoples in Bolivia today, other tribes still survive, like the Puquina-speaking Indians, whose numbers have dwindled drastically over the centuries. A few hundred descendants of the pre-Columbian Chipaya Indians, who shared the altiplano with the Aymara, live in the arid Carangas region west of Lake Poopó. They survive mainly

Bolivians gather in a plaza to watch the Eighth of August Independence Day parade in Potosí. Whereas the stovepipe hat is characteristic of the Potosí region, the bowler, the fedora, and even the baseball cap also appear there, reflecting the relatively recent redistributions of native cultures throughout the country.

by trading llamas, sheep's milk, and cheese to the Aymara in exchange for potatoes and quinoa, the Aymara's chief crops. The Uru, a once-numerous pre-Columbian tribe that lived around Lakes Titicaca and Poopó, apparently have disappeared as a distinct people. According to one anthropologist, the last person of pure Uru ancestry died in 1960. Both the Uru and the Chipaya have intermarried with the Aymara, and their cultures have blended with the Aymara culture.

The Callahuaya, another important Indian group, was originally part of the Aymara culture but has long considered itself to be a separate, distinct people. The Callahuaya enjoyed a special status among the altiplano Indians as peddlers of charms and magical or curative potions. Their success with medicine supposedly earned them the role of court physicians to the Inca emperors. Some historians believe they are the ones who introduced the use of quinine, a medicine that is derived from tree bark and combats malaria, to the Spaniards.

Numerous small groups of Indians live in the thinly populated rain forest and lowland plains of the Oriente. Descended from the original Arawakan and Guaraní tribes as well as from some 40 much smaller tribes, they are scattered throughout the region, living for the most part in great poverty. Other Indians moved to the Oriente from the highlands and valleys after the 1952 revolution in an attempt to develop the less-populated Oriente. They continue to practice subsistence farming or commercial agriculture.

Cholos, Mestizos, and Blancos

Nearly one-third of the Bolivian population is made up of people of mixed Indian and European heritage. They are cholos or mestizos. "Cholo" is the word used to refer to an upwardly mobile, lower-class urban dweller; some cholos are not of mixed heritage but are Indians who have moved to the city and taken on the ways of the mestizos.

An altiplano woman prepares breakfast for her family. Most members of the family—including children—drink coffee at breakfast.

The mestizo, on the other hand, is always a person of mixed Indian and European ancestry. Many mestizos have professional positions as doctors, university professors, or engineers. As a rule, mestizos are usually better off financially than cholos, and some successful or prominent mestizos are accepted as *blancos*, or members of the white elite. Regardless of their standing, though, mestizos and cholos usually have some level of education and can read and write as well as speak Spanish. To a large extent they constitute the urban work force of the Bolivian economy.

Some blancos are the descendants of the Spanish settlers who came to South America during the colonial period. Others, like former president Germán Busch, are the offspring of German immigrants who came to the country in the late 19th and early 20th centuries, during Bolivia's tin rush. Others have descended from German Jews who fled Nazi persecution in the 1930s and 1940s, although after World War II Bolivia offered haven to Nazis as well.

The city of Santa Cruz, in the southern Oriente, is an oasis of Spanish culture and is one of the few places in Bolivia where the white population equals the Indian. For centuries severed from the rest of the country by impenetrable terrain and lack of good roads, Santa Cruz remained predominantly Spanish, with little intermarriage or interaction between the whites and the Indians. Today it is the fastest-growing city in Bolivia and counts among its inhabitants an increasing number of Indians from the highlands and Peru as well as a small population of foreigners of non-European descent. Among the recent immigrants to the area have been several thousand Japanese, who emigrated to the country in the 1950s and have been leaders in the development of the commercial fruit and vegetable industry. Several thousand Dutch-Canadian Mennonites have also settled in the region. Arabs from Lebanon, Syria, and Palestine have also settled in Bolivia although not just in the Santa Cruz area.

Education and Health

In a land where one-third of the people over 15 years of age cannot read or write, education is seen as essential to Bolivia's social and economic development. The government provides free elementary and secondary school education, and the law says that all children between the ages of 6 and 14 must attend. However, some communities lack the necessary schools; also, rural children frequently drop out before they reach the age of 14 to help in the fields. Today about 82 percent of the school-age children attend school and the number of enrollments has greatly increased since 1952, when the figure was 15 percent.

Bolivia has 10 colleges and universities, virtually all of them located in the country's major cities. The oldest, the University of

(continued on page 73)

SCENES OF
BOLIVIA

Overleaf: Bolivian children work with domesticated llamas on a farm near Lake Titicaca.

The figure of Viracocha, the creator lord of the people of Tiahuanaco and their descendants, the Aymara Indians, towers over the doorway of the Gate of the Sun, which was made around A.D. 600. The civilization of the ancient city of Tiahuanaco was one of the most advanced Indian cultures of its time.

On Lake Titicaca, an Indian paddles a balsa, *a banana-shaped boat made from reeds.*

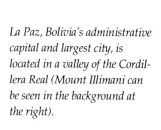

La Paz, Bolivia's administrative capital and largest city, is located in a valley of the Cordillera Real (Mount Illimani can be seen in the background at the right).

Two Bolivians place a bouquet of flowers at the grave of a family member in a cemetery in La Paz.

The Supreme Court building lies beyond an ornate fountain in Sucre, the judicial capital of Bolivia. Sucre is perhaps the Bolivian city most steeped in the history of its Spanish past.

A vendor sells woven articles in La Paz. Folk art such as weaving and knitting is made by local artisans and sold primarily to Indians and tourists.

A local vendor peddles various herbs and peppers at a market in La Paz.

A street scene in the historical section of La Paz harks back to the Spanish colonial era when wrought-iron balconies and whitewashed mansions pervaded the city.

A potter shapes bowls in his workshop in Cochabamba.

Workers at a Karachipampa mineral refinery take a break from their labors to listen to a speech. Bolivia is one of the world's leading exporters of minerals.

An Indian woman from the town of Tarabuco, southeast of Sucre, wears such traditional clothes as a handwoven cape and hat.

(continued from page 65)
San Francisco Xavier in Sucre, was founded in 1624. During the Spanish colonial period, it was one of the most influential schools in Latin America. There the revolutionaries of the early 1800s cultivated the ideas that would lead them to declare their independence from Spain in 1809. The University of San Andrés, in La Paz, is the nation's largest, with a student population of about 20,000.

Although only about 5 percent of adults 25 years of age or older have attended college, a significant number of these graduates leave Bolivia for more lucrative jobs in Argentina, Chile, and elsewhere in South America. This exodus of Bolivia's educated professionals has drained the country of much-needed skills and has hindered its economic development. For example, there is only 1 doctor for every 2,600 persons in Bolivia, and most of the nation's health care givers are concentrated in the major cities. This means that the half

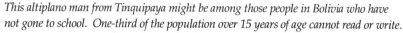

This altiplano man from Tinquipaya might be among those people in Bolivia who have not gone to school. One-third of the population over 15 years of age cannot read or write.

Whereas the division of labor still falls along traditional gender-proscribed roles, some women have become successful professionals. This mestizo woman is an architect in La Paz.

of the population that lives in rural areas does not have the same degree of access to medical care as do city dwellers.

Since the revolution of 1952, the government has established health clinics in some rural communities, but these services are still few and far between. Frequently the facilities go unused anyway, because many Indians still rely on traditional practices to cure ailments and ward off disease. They turn to the *yatiri*, or folk doctor, and his time-honored selection of potions and rituals, which he usually dispenses after reading the coca leaves to determine his diagnosis.

Next to malnutrition and infant diseases, Bolivia's biggest health problem is poor sanitation. Inadequate sewage disposal and poor hygiene are common causes of sickness, notably intestinal disorders and diseases spread by flies and other insects. In the humid jungles of eastern Bolivia, mosquitoes transmit diseases such as malaria and yellow fever. The mines, too, have their health hazards. Tuberculosis and silicosis (lung diseases) are especially prevalent among miners, as is death or disability from accident.

Despite the progress Bolivia has made since 1952, it remains one of the least developed countries in South America, both socially and economically. But because economic and social development often go hand in hand, with one feeding the other, it is unlikely that the government, without economic growth, will be able to build the schools and health care facilities that are so desperately needed. And without education and some measure of integration, it is unlikely that the various groups within society will unite to form an economically strong Bolivia that can serve the needs of all its citizens.

Although mining employs only three percent of the population, it continues to be one of Bolivia's biggest sources of income, and the miner's union is very powerful.

7

The Economy

Perhaps nowhere in Bolivia is the contrast between old and new, and between Indian and European, more apparent than in the Bolivian economy. Subsistence farming, the Indians' traditional form of labor, occupies nearly half the country's workers but does not come near to supplying Bolivia's food requirements and contributes little to the economy. Conversely, mining, the backbone of the economy since Spanish times and the nation's chief source of exportable goods, employs less than five percent of all workers. These two industries symbolize the cultural differences that have divided the country for four centuries. The community-based Indian economy has traditionally emphasized working the land together and sharing the bounty of the harvest, while the cash-based Spanish economy introduced the concepts of private property, consumption of material goods, and individual enterprise.

Agriculture: The Focus of Indian Life

The roots of agriculture go back thousands of years in Bolivia, at least as far as the Tiahuanaco culture. When the Aymara ruled the altiplano in the 14th century, each ayllu worked the land communally, and extensive trade networks between the highlands and lowlands provided the Indians of each region with a variety of goods. Later, when the Inca conquered the Aymara, they further developed this system of communal farming. The Inca divided each ayllu into three sections: one for the Inca emperor, one for the sun god, and one for the ayllu. Everyone had to work the fields of the Inca and the sun god. The harvest from these fields went to feed the royal family, other nobles, the empire's army, and the religious leaders. The crops for official use were stored in warehouses, as were any surplus crops, and the reserves from these warehouses (which were said to hold several years' supply of food) provided emergency relief should the harvest fail in any part of the empire.

Today, most Indians follow traditional farming practices. They use hand-held wooden implements to farm small tracts of land, and oxen still pull crude plows through the stony earth. The barter system of exchange is still widely used throughout the countryside and in the Indian quarter of many cities. Even the smallest towns usually have their weekly market, where Indians trade their surplus crops for other goods.

Most of the country's farming takes place on the altiplano, especially around Lake Titicaca, where the soil is more fertile and the rainfall more abundant, but only the hardiest of crops can withstand the rigorous climate of the high plateau. Among those are barley, quinoa, *oca* (a small, slender root similar to a potato and native to the altiplano), and the all-important potato, some 220 varieties of which are grown in Bolivia. (As a testament to the potato's importance, the Aymara language has at least 200 different words to describe the various types.) The potato was first domesticated on these wild, windy highlands and was introduced to the rest of the world by the Spanish, who shipped it back to their native country. From there it spread through Europe and to virtually every part of the globe.

Around Lake Titicaca, the milder climate supports less hardy crops, such as wheat, beans, and corn. These crops are also grown in the Yungas and Valles east of the altiplano, as are a host of fruits and vegetables, among them bananas, oranges, turnips, carrots, and cassava, which is used to make tapioca. Sugarcane, coffee, cocoa, and rice are also important products of this region.

Because the agriculture of the altiplano is mostly subsistence farming, the valleys have become the center of Bolivia's commercial agriculture industry and now provide much of the food consumed in the cities. The fertile plains around Santa Cruz, in the southeastern Oriente, have been an important farming region since the 1950s, when construction of a highway between Santa Cruz and Cochabamba made trade with the region practical. Among the chief products grown there are citrus fruits, cotton, tea, coffee, sugarcane, and rice. The latter three are leaders among the few agricultural products Bolivia exports.

The rest of the Oriente affords little agriculture, except for Brazil nuts and latex in the northern rain forest. Latex, the substance used to make rubber, was at one time a major export. But in 1903, the country lost its richest latex-producing region when Brazilians who had settled in that territory revolted against Bolivian rule and forced

A market woman sells bread dolls for the Day of the Dead celebration. These get placed at the graves of family members.

Women pick through the leftover tin ore to supplement the family income. Bolivia is one of the world's leading producers of tin.

the country to cede an area of 189,000 square miles (489,637 square kilometers) to Brazil in the largest land loss in Bolivia's history. Today, most of the northern Oriente's vast acreage is devoted to cattle ranching. The grassy plains that cover much of the territory provide ideal grazing lands, and beef from the Oriente is exported to Peru and Brazil. However, the largest market for Bolivian-raised beef is Bolivia itself.

The llama, alpaca, and vicuña served as the Andean Indians' principal beasts of burden and their primary sources of wool before the Spaniards introduced mules, oxen, and sheep in the 16th century. Indeed, these cousins of the camel were so highly prized in prehistoric Aymara society that they lived in the same house as the family. Indians today still regard their animals as a sign of wealth and prestige (a large herd means a wealthy owner), although sometimes this practice leads to the amassing of herds that are larger than is financially necessary or practical. Today, however, sheep mingle placidly with the flocks of llama and alpaca grazing leisurely on the altiplano, and chickens, pigs, and goats, relative newcomers to the region, amble freely around the clusters of adobe houses.

Silver, Gold, and the Devil's Metal

In Inca times, mining was a minor activity carried out to adorn the emperors' clothing and buildings. By the 16th century, visions of great wealth lured Spanish colonists to the forlorn altiplano, as the silver hill at Potosí fed the coffers and dreams of many a fortune seeker. In its day Potosí was the best-known city in the New World, and its cobbled streets bustled with richly clothed Spaniards dressed in silk and satin garments.

But by the mid-18th century, Potosí's treasures had been all but exhausted, and the imperial city that had once commanded the attention of the entire world tumbled into decline. The city made something of a comeback after the tin boom of the late 19th century, but "the devil's metal," as tin is called in Bolivia, did not renew Potosí's fame. By this time the center of the Bolivian mining industry had shifted northward to the towns of Oruro and Uncía.

Today, Oruro and Uncía are the heart of Bolivia's mining industry. The region in which they are found is commonly called the tin belt because it contains the bulk of the nation's tin deposits. Tin is the country's chief export, and Bolivia is one of the world's leading producers of the metal. Since the nationalization of the three biggest tin mines in 1952, most of the tin industry has been controlled by the state-run mining corporation, COMIBOL. The government takeover of the mines has not, however, created the kind of progress that had been expected. The company has been plagued by labor strikes and inefficient equipment and management, and a lack of money for development has kept it from exploring for new deposits. In addition to COMIBOL, there are a growing number of medium-sized privately owned mines whose output of minerals has been steadily, if slowly, increasing. These companies extract tin as well as antimony, tungsten, lead, copper, zinc, silver, and bismuth. Gold is panned primarily in the western rivers in Beni and is also among Bolivia's mineral exports.

Oil in the Oriente

Since it was first developed in the early 1920s by the United States–owned Standard Oil Company of Bolivia, the petroleum industry has witnessed a series of starts and stops. In 1937, the Bolivian government confiscated the company and created the state-owned Bolivian National Oilfields Company, or YPFB, but this organization lacked both experienced technicians and funds for exploration. After 1952, the revolutionary government poured money into YPFB and opened the country to foreign developers. By the 1960s, Bolivia was producing enough oil to fulfill its own needs and was even exporting a small amount. Then, in 1969, the government again nationalized the principal foreign-owned company in Bolivia,

Large petroleum towers dominate this state-owned refinery in Santa Cruz.

which at that time was the Gulf Oil Company. Only a few years later, however, foreigners were again invited to develop the country's petroleum resources.

Although Bolivia's hopes for developing a strong petroleum industry to balance its dependence on tin mining have not borne fruit, another resource, natural gas, has proved much more promising. Natural gas ranks second to tin as the country's main export (together the two products account for nearly three-fourths of all exports). Bolivia itself uses very little natural gas and ships most of it across the border to Argentina and Brazil.

The Manufacturing and Service Industries

About 10 percent of the total work force is employed in manufacturing, which for the most part revolves around industries that process the various minerals mined in Bolivia. These include tin and antimony smelters, oil refineries, and plants that produce petrochemicals (chemicals derived from petroleum or natural gas). Other factories process agricultural products, such as sugar, coffee, or rice. The majority of these industries are located in La Paz, Santa Cruz, and Cochabamba, Bolivia's three largest cities.

A few of Bolivia's factories produce textiles and clothing for sale within the country. Individual craftspeople and artisans also make clothing, pottery, and jewelry; these articles are generally traded in the Indian markets or sold to tourists.

About 34 percent of the labor force holds jobs in service industries—that is, jobs that provide some sort of service to the public. These people work in schools, businesses, hotels, hospitals, insurance companies, banks, and government offices.

Transportation and Communications

Like the mining and petroleum industries, most of Bolivia's transportation industry is owned by the government. Railroads link all of the major cities, but because of the country's arduous terrain, the transportation network is not widely developed. A rail

A literal cliff-hanger of a road winds its way across the eastern cordillera between La Paz and the Yungas.

route between La Paz and the Chilean ports of Antofagasta and Arica carries Bolivian goods to the Pacific Ocean for shipment worldwide. Likewise, systems in the south and east link up with Brazilian and Argentinean lines to provide outlets to the Atlantic coast.

The roadway system in Bolivia is even less extensive than the railway system. Most of the roads are located in the highlands, because frequent flooding of the lowlands makes road building there impractical. The one major thoroughfare in the Oriente is the 308-mile (497-kilometer) highway between Santa Cruz and Cochabamba. Built in the 1950s after the national revolution, this paved roadway has been a key element in the rapid development of the Santa Cruz region. Many of the roads in the highlands are little more than one-lane trails, spiraling paths hacked out of the edge of the cordillera at death-defying angles and curves. Although the country has only 1 car for every 150 persons, Bolivians make the most of their transportation. Often a dozen or more will be crowded into the back of an old pickup truck on its way to or from the market, their goods slung on their backs and their hats bobbing in accompaniment to the rhythm of the vehicle's well-worn shocks.

The easiest way to navigate Bolivia's rugged terrain is by air. The Bolivian airline, Lloyd Aéreo Boliviano (LAB), flies to many Bolivian cities as well as to major cities within Latin America. La Paz has the distinction of possessing the world's highest-altitude commercial airport, at 12,001 feet (3,637 meters) above sea level. It is open to international flights, as are Cochabamba and Santa Cruz.

In addition to air transportation, the major cities are connected by telephone systems. Most of the rural areas do not have access to this service, because the majority of the country homes are not wired for electricity. For this reason also, many people do not own televisions. Radios, however, are common and are one of the few manufactured items that Indians are eager to buy.

Banking and International Trade

Although there are private banks in Bolivia (most of which are owned by foreign firms), the largest and most important banks in the country are owned by the government. These include Banco Mineral (Mineral Bank), Banco Agricola (Agricultural Bank), and Banco Central (Central Bank). This last institution serves as the

This airport in La Paz has the highest altitude of any commercial airport in the world.

Campesinos till a coca field in the Yunga Valley. The vastness of the plantation can be gauged by comparing the farmer in the foreground with the one at the lower left.

government's bank and issues the nation's currency. The basic unit of currency is the peso boliviano.

Bolivia maintains trade with many foreign countries. Its principal trade partners are the United States, Japan, Brazil, Argentina, and West Germany. In addition, the country belongs to the Andean Pact, a five-member organization (the other members are Venezuela, Colombia, Ecuador, and Peru) whose participants share a common market. These countries have a special trade relationship with each other, and goods produced by member nations have preference over goods produced by nonmember nations.

The Armed Forces

Throughout Bolivia's history as a republic, the military has played a central role in the country's evolution. Often it has been the ruling power, and once, after the national revolution in the early 1950s, it was all but disbanded. Today, Bolivia maintains a 20,000-man army as well as a small air force and navy. All males between the ages of

19 and 49 are required to serve for a year in one of the armed services, and men of military age can be drafted in times of national emergency.

The Coca "Industry"

It is widely believed that coca tops tin on the list of Bolivian exports—but the sale of this product outside Bolivia is illegal, so nobody knows exactly how much is grown or exported. Bolivia is the second leading producer of coca leaves, after Peru. Most of the coca leaves that are produced in Bolivia are grown in the Yungas, northeast of Cochabamba. After harvesting, the leaves are turned into a paste in illicit laboratories deep in the Oriente's northwestern jungles. Then the paste is shipped to Colombia, the base of the major cocaine trafficking rings, for final processing and distribution.

Though in the past the Bolivian government has been linked to the underground coca trade, recent administrations have tried to stem the flourishing industry. In 1986, U.S. soldiers helped Bolivian drug police destroy many of the secret laboratories that refine the coca leaves into paste. This operation temporarily halted the export of coca from Bolivia, but within a few months coca paste was again flowing out of the country.

Because the peasant farmers who raise the leaves can make so much more money from coca than from other crops, some leaders in Bolivia argue that the coca trade will not be eliminated until the Indians can earn as much from legal crops. They say that the emphasis should be not on wiping out the trade by force but on educating the farmers to the dangers of coca and encouraging them to grow other crops, which would also increase the nation's domestic food supply. But in a nation that continues to be one of the poorest and least educated in South America, coca production—despite its social and legal hazards—can appear compellingly attractive to people who live in poverty and are hungry every day.

The church in Copacabana is a relic of the Spanish colonial era.

8

Religion, Culture, and the Arts

Bolivia is the most "Indian" of the South American countries. Although its culture is a fascinating blend of old and new, of Indian and European, the Indian influence has remained stronger here than in other countries, and the percentage of the population that is of unmixed Indian descent is higher than elsewhere in South America.

Yet Bolivia has different cultures that reflect its different social classes. Thus, most Bolivians in the countryside wear Indian clothing, live in earthen houses, and perform ceremonies to Indian gods, while in the cities many people dress in blue jeans and T-shirts, live in high-rise apartments or modern houses, and worship in Christian churches. Even in the cities, however, there are distinct cultural differences between the cholos and the blancos. Furthermore, each of the cities is itself distinctive.

Discovering Bolivia's Major Cities

La Paz, with nearly 1 million inhabitants, is by far the largest and most modern city in Bolivia. It seems to tumble from the edge of the eastern altiplano into a basin below. The dimensions of La Paz seem to change daily as it struggles to keep up with the influx of newcomers from the countryside and to maintain its reputation as an international city. Because of its narrow confines, the city grows vertically more than horizontally, shooting up onto the altiplano high above the town center as well as spilling down into the bottom of the basin and onto the other side of the embankment.

La Paz neighborhoods are strictly divided according to class. On the steep slopes above the city live the cholos, their one- or two-room adobe huts clinging precariously to the hillside. Life here is lived in the streets, which serve as offices, shops, and social gathering spots. Indian women, their wares spread on the ground before them, line the roadsides that crisscross the upper slopes, while busloads of Indians shuttling to or from the downtown area navigate the winding streets.

Farther down the hillside, toward the center of town, the city's mestizo population live in homes made from bricks of sun-baked earth covered with a thin layer of plaster. Here the highway leading down from El Alto Airport into La Paz changes names several times and eventually becomes Avenida 16 de Julio, the main avenue of the city. The street, which for three of its blocks is known as El Prado, divides downtown La Paz into two sections. The north section is considered the historical center of the city. It contains the 19th-century Cathedral of La Paz, the presidential palace, and the lamppost from which President Villarroel was lynched in 1946.

The geographic center and heartbeat of the city is located south of El Prado, however. Here, throngs of cholos crowd the narrow cobbled streets among the sidewalk vendors and shopkeepers. One of the most crowded and fascinating streets in this section is Calle Linares, where people buy charms, potions, coca leaves, and other remedies prescribed by their local yatiri. These streets are lined with small shops that sell handmade items, such as knitted sweaters, silver jewelry, and musical instruments. One block north

Near the turn of the century, highlanders herd llamas through a La Paz street.

of El Prado, at the open-air market known as the Mercado Camacho, market women reign over stalls piled high with fruits, vegetables, and meat, eagerly prodding potential customers to buy their goods.

As El Prado changes names once again and winds its way south and back into the suburbs, the neighborhoods take on a different look. This is the wealthy section of La Paz, where the city's elite and foreign officials live, and the houses here are larger and more elegant. The people speak Spanish, and signs of Bolivia's colonial past still linger in the enclosed patios that reflect the imprint of Spanish architecture.

Perhaps nowhere are Bolivia's Spanish roots more evident, however, than in Sucre, the constitutional capital of the country. Everything about this city of 80,000 speaks of a bygone era. Beneath the low-hanging eaves of brick red tile and the wrought-iron balconies laced with geraniums and bougainvillea lies a world preserved from earlier days. Inside the whitewashed mansions that border the smooth streets of stone, the treasures of the old colonial aristocracy still fill the faded rooms. The 1952 revolution and the subsequent agricultural reform changed forever the fortunes of Sucre's elite, but the remaining residents still cling tenaciously to their old ways.

By contrast, Santa Cruz is a boomtown that cannot keep pace with the present. The second-largest city in Bolivia, it is also the fastest growing, with a population of more than 400,000. Since the early 1950s, when the highway connecting it with Cochabamba was completed, the population of Santa Cruz and its environs have grown at least tenfold. Santa Cruz promises to continue its rapid rate of development. For years a crude frontier settlement cut off from the rest of the country, the city is now the hub of Bolivia's oil industry and an important agricultural center (as well as the preferred residence of Bolivia's cocaine barons). Much of the old town, with its wooden verandas and mud-packed streets, has been replaced by modern structures.

Cochabamba, tucked in the folds of the eastern cordillera, is an up-and-coming metropolis pulsating with activity. It is Bolivia's third-largest city. Flowers bloom year-round in the springlike climate the city enjoys. Like Sucre, Cochabamba is steeped in the history of its Spanish past, but the mood here is not as placid as in the old capital. This city of 304,000 has its sights firmly set on the future, and one gets the feeling that its residents grow impatient with the slow march of progress. Although there are canning and shoe factories in Cochabamba, its most important industry is agriculture. For centuries, produce plucked from the fertile hills surrounding Cochabamba has fed the people in the highland cities. Perhaps nowhere else in Bolivia can such a variety of food be found.

Eating and Drinking the Bolivian Way

The traditional Bolivian diet centers on potatoes, quinoa, and beans, all of which were domesticated in the Americas thousands of years ago. Unlike many other Indian cultures, in which corn is the chief crop, the Indians of Bolivia have depended on the potato. It is their most important food, and more varieties of potatoes can be found in the Andes than anywhere else in the world.

The highland Indians have about as many ways of eating potatoes as they do varieties of them. Potatoes are most often freeze-dried by exposure to the cold, dry air of the altiplano (these potatoes are called *chuños*). These dehydrated potatoes can be stored for years; the Incas filled their warehouses with chuños to guard against famine. Often they are added to soups or stews, but they can also be eaten alone and have a distinctive and pleasing flavor.

Quinoa, a high-protein grain related to millet, was second only to the potato as the Inca's most important food. Today it remains a staple of the Indians' diet. It is frequently boiled into porridge or ground into flour. Fermented, it becomes *chicha*, a beer consumed by almost all the highland Indians.

A homemade brand of beer, called chicha, *is usually made from corn. The brewers, mostly women, chew the corn and spit it into enormous vats. The mixture is heated and then ferments.*

In the cities, the basic diet of potatoes, beans, and quinoa gives way to a wider variety of foods and dishes. *Salteñas*, spicy pastries filled with meat and vegetables, can be found in almost all Bolivian cities and are a sort of national food, much like hot dogs in the United States. They are usually served piping hot as a midmorning snack. *Empanadas* are another popular meat-filled pastry, though they are often stuffed with cheese instead of meat. Like salteñas, they taste best when they are eaten straight from the oven.

Chewing the coca leaf is part of traditional Indian life. Coca's anesthetic effect helps the ill-fed and often insufficiently clad Indians subdue their pangs of hunger and withstand the frigid climate of the altiplano. Many people believe the plant to have magical qualities, and its leaves are frequently studied as omens of the future. They are also prescribed to relieve the unpleasant effects of *soroche*, or altitude sickness, an ailment that often afflicts newcomers unaccustomed to the extreme heights.

Coca is also part of Indian mythology. According to legend, the ancestors of the altiplano Indians descended into the valleys of the Yungas in search of new land. Because they found this land covered with dense forests, the Indians set fire to the area to strip the land of its trees and to uncover the fertile soil. But the fire raged out of control and the smoke made its way to the storm god. This god was so angry that he unleashed a violent storm, which extinguished the fire but exterminated all plant life as well. Only the coca plant survived the storm god's wrath. The Indians, weak with hunger, quickly devoured its leaves and immediately felt their strength restored.

Bolivia produces some distinctive national beverages. Among them are *singani*, a whiskey made from white grapes that grow around Tarija, and chicha, which can be made from quinoa and various fruits but is usually made from corn. This sour beer can be found throughout the highlands and valleys. Aymara Indians were drinking chicha before the Inca ever descended upon Bolivia, and it is still an important component of many traditional Indian rituals. No Indian will drink a glass of the brew without first pouring a few drops on the ground as an offering to Pachamama, the earth mother. This ancient practice, known as *cha'llar*, was always performed at planting time to ensure a successful harvest. Because agriculture continues to play such a central role in their lives, Indians still observe this and many other ancient customs, although today these customs have usually merged with Christian religious celebrations.

Christian Saints and Indian Supayas

Although the primary god of the Inca empire was the sun, Inti, the Inca worshiped many other gods and goddesses as well, among them Pachamama, Illampu (the storm god), and Mama Cocha (Mother Sea). Because the Inca culture revolved around agriculture, anything having to do with farming was considered holy, and religious celebrations tended to be tied to the agricultural cycle of planting, ripening, and harvesting. The Inca emperor himself planted the first seeds of corn each August, and ceremonies were performed throughout the year to attract rain, give thanks for water, and honor the new plants. At harvest time in May and June, Indians throughout the empire held thanksgiving festivals to celebrate the successful season.

The Aymara, too, worshipped numerous gods, including their creator Viracocha, Pachamama, and Supay, an evil spirit who lived in the earth. However, when the conquistadores arrived in the early 16th century, they declared all Indian gods and goddesses to be *supayas*, or evil spirits, and began a rigorous program of converting the Quechua and Aymara to Roman Catholicism, the official religion of Spain. Although outwardly the Spanish appear to have succeeded in their mission (95 percent of all Bolivians are Catholic), in reality most of the Indians and many cholos and mestizos still recognize their traditional gods as well. Some of these gods and goddesses have been fused with Christian figures; for example,

A statue of the Virgin Mary is being removed from a church in Potosí. It will be paraded through the streets during the Feast of Our Lady.

Pachamama is often associated with the Virgin Mary and the sun god Inti with Jesus.

Indian festivals, too, have blended with Christianity. Now on June 24, instead of Inti Raymi, the Festival of the Sun, the Indians celebrate St. John's Day—but they retain many of the original Inti Raymi rituals. Traditionally, during this festival the Inca lit a sacrificial fire in the Temple of the Sun to celebrate the winter solstice (June 22), which is the longest night of the year in the Southern Hemisphere. Today, the mountains still glow with light on St. John's Eve, as people all over the highlands burn bonfires to bring back the sun. The lighting of fires on St. John's Day also has Christian significance, for, according to legend, Elizabeth, the mother of John the Baptist, had fires lit across Israel to inform the Virgin Mary that John had been born.

In November, the month during which the Inca honored the dead, the Indians now perform their ancient rituals on the Christian feasts of All Saints' Day and All Souls' Day, November 1 and 2. They place food and drink around the graves of their ancestors and offer miniature boats and ladders to help the dead cross over into the afterlife. It is not a somber day; frequently the entire community turns out to celebrate with music and dancing.

The liveliest and most spectacular festival, however, is the Carnaval, which takes place in February or March, just before the Christian season of Lent. Almost all major Bolivian cities stage week-long celebrations, but the town best known for its Carnaval is Oruro, because of its *diablada*, or devil dance, which depicts the victory of good over evil. The men who dance the diablada, usually miners or railroad workers, are for three days the stars of the Carnaval, performing intricately choreographed dance steps for hours on end. The dancers wear elaborately embroidered breastplates trimmed with stones and silver fringe; short capes swirl around their shoulders. But their lavish clothes almost go unnoticed under the grotesque plaster masks that top each costume. Here is the devil incarnate, with bulging eyes, silver fangs, twisted

Masked dancers perform at a celebration of Bolivian native cultures.

horns, and writhing reptiles, all wildly painted in a kaleidoscope of colors.

Throughout the day, the dance groups weave their way up to the church at the entrance to the Oruro mine. They remove their masks and approach the altar, where they sing to the Virgin of the Mines and are blessed by the priest. At dawn the following day, the devil dancers again return to the church for mass and then proceed to an open area, where they perform an expanded version of the diablada.

The Carnaval celebration continues throughout the week, with water fights, eating, drinking, and dancing. Some of the dances may go on for hours, the participants weaving and twirling in a mesmerizing motion to music from a local band. The popular *cueca*, a Spanish courtship dance, is a standard at almost all festivities, and frequently Bolivians will bid each other farewell by singing or dancing the *kacharpaya*.

But music and dancing are not confined to Bolivia's numerous holidays. Many of the large cities, especially La Paz, feature traditional folk music in *las peñas*, or clubs. Several nights each week patrons listen to the haunting melodies of the Andean highlands performed on such traditional Indian instruments as the wooden *tarka* (a square, six-holed flute), the high-pitched *charango* (an instrument similar to a ukulele and made from an armadillo shell), and the *zampoña*, or panpipes.

Art and Literature

For much of Bolivia's early and postconquest history, art was meant to adorn clothing, utensils, and churches rather than to stand alone as an expression of the artist's skill. Thus, much of Bolivia's best art is found not in museums or art galleries (though Bolivia has several of these) but in the streets and meeting places of everyday life; in the ancient relics of Tiahuanaco; in the numerous ornate colonial churches that are found in almost every highland city; and in the

A woman weaves colorful cloth on a large loom; the cloth is cut into smaller sizes and made into blankets or shawls.

superbly crafted handmade items that are commonly found in the Indian shops and markets.

Some of the most prized items are found in the tumbledown foundations that once were parts of prehistoric cities. Scattered throughout the Yungas are the remains of various stone fortresses that guarded the frontiers of the Inca empire from attack by lowland tribes. The Inca were well known for their beautifully crafted objects of silver and gold. For the Incas, these metals were purely ornamental and were often used for ceremonial purposes. As the son of the sun (and thus divine in his own right), the Inca emperor wore clothes trimmed with gold, ate off gold plates, lived in gold-plated buildings, and walked in a garden filled with life-size llamas and ears of corn made of solid gold. Most of the Inca's beautiful objects of precious metal, however, were destroyed along with the

Local musicians parade through the street of Tinquipaya during Carnaval.

empire, their golden forms melted down into ingots and shipped to Spain to fill the royal treasury.

Paintings, sculptures, and carvings from the colonial period frame the altars and adorn the spires of the dozens of churches the Spanish built. The Spanish brought to Bolivia the styles of art then popular in Spain, but because there were so few European artists in the colonies, the Spaniards had to rely on mestizos who had apprenticed under European masters. The mestizo baroque style of painting and architecture evolved from this mix in the 17th and 18th centuries, combining Spanish techniques with traditional Indian forms. The 18th-century church of San Francisco, in the heart of La Paz, is a good example of the mestizo baroque style, as is the Merced church in Sucre, which features 35 pictures by Melchor Pérez Holguin, the foremost painter of that period.

Folk art is the most visible and most enduring art to be found in Bolivia. Woven and knitted articles, silver jewelry, pottery, and other handicrafts are made by local artisans and sold primarily to

Indians or tourists. The Inca were some of the finest weavers in all of the Americas, and this art form is still practiced in much the same manner as it was 500 years ago, with men weaving the large pieces of fabric and women weaving the smaller pieces and dying the wool. Garments ranging from belts to ponchos to *aguayos* (shawls that are also used to carry produce or children) still display the traditional bird, animal, and dancer designs that were found in Inca times. Each highland district has its own traditional colors. Although most of the clothing worn by the Indians is woven, not knitted, the Indians are also excellent knitters and are well known for their soft silky sweaters and hats made from alpaca or sheep's wool.

Bolivian folk artists have a particular talent for miniatures. This art is directly related to one of the country's major festivities, the Alacitas fair, which is held to honor Ekeko, the dwarflike god of prosperity and good fortune. During the fair, people buy miniatures of whatever they want in the coming year. All kinds of miniatures can be had here, from kitchens to groceries to farm animals to presidential palaces. Statues of the stout, mustached god in whose name this fair is held can be found in almost every Indian household, for in addition to being the bearer of good luck he is also the god of marriage.

The literary arts in Bolivia are not as well developed as the fine and folk arts, but the country has produced a number of noted writers and poets, many of whom emerged after the ruinous Chaco War. Among the best known are Augusto Céspedes, whose novel *Metal del Diablo* (The Devil's Metal) is based on the life of Bolivian tin baron Simón Patiño, and Jesús Lara, whose works about the Indian peasants have been published outside the country. The great Bolivian poet Franz Tamayo also wrote about the Andean Indian culture, claiming that "the greatness of a race is directly proportionate to the difficulties it has overcome."

The present generation of children, such as these students from Tarija, have been raised in an era of toppling governments and economic crises. Bolivia's future lies in its ability to reform and stabilize its government and economy.

Toward the 21st Century

There are signs that for all its stormy past, Bolivia is finally evolving into the modern democratic country that Simón Bolívar hoped it would become. But modernization does not necessarily mean Westernization or Americanization, as the leaders of Bolivia are learning. Modernization means unifying a long-divided population by recognizing the Indians and cholos as full-fledged members of the society to which their cultures have made important contributions throughout Bolivia's history.

Change occurs slowly in Bolivia. Old patterns of thinking die hard, but real progress can be made only when the ultimate goal is not to exchange the culture of one people for another but to benefit from both cultures.

Some progress has been achieved in Bolivia. The revolution of 1952 turned Bolivian society upside down and altered the republic forever. Virtually all the Indians who wanted to own land now possess their own farms. And the government's efforts to attract farmers to the Oriente have met with some success: The region around Santa Cruz is now one of the country's major agricultural centers.

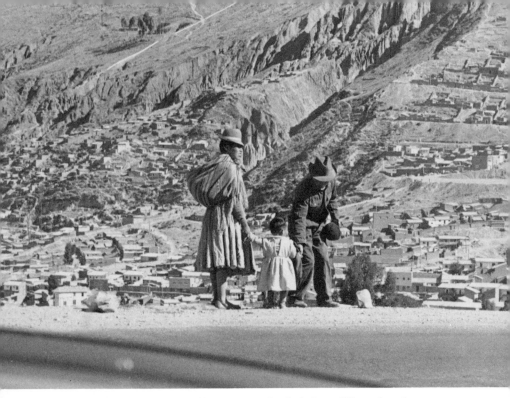

The immediate future for the Bolivian peasant family looks no different from its present, but thousands of years of history testify to its ability to survive.

Bolivia's mining industry also shows promise. The development of the Oriente's natural-gas reserves has helped to ease the country's dependence on tin, and recent discoveries of iron ore in the southeast region may provide yet another source of much-needed foreign income. Estimates suggest that only about five percent of the nation's deposits have been discovered—but the high altitudes at which most minerals are found, and the lack of funds to develop new mines, have so far kept Bolivia from tapping into its remaining deposits.

Meanwhile, the cocaine industry poses a serious dilemma. Already, several Bolivian drug rings have emerged to compete with the Colombian cartels that dominate the international distribution of the drug. Bolivia has built several new helicopter bases in the northern jungles and developed the Rural Police Force in order to stamp out the illicit drug trade, but these measures are still in their infancy. Today, the cocaine trade is in danger of disrupting the fragile workings of the civilian government.

That Bolivia has survived for so long without being swallowed by its powerful neighbors or being torn apart internally is truly a remarkable thing. When one considers the political, social, and economic turmoil that has plagued the country for nearly 300 years, the words of Simón Bolívar still ring true today: "The more I think about the destiny of the country," he said, "the more it seems to me a tiny marvel."

GLOSSARY

altiplano   A Spanish word for the high plateau that separates the two Andean mountain ranges of Bolivia. Historically the center of Andean Indian life, the altiplano contains the majority of Bolivia's population.

ayllu   A community made up of extended family members. The ayllu was the cornerstone of Aymara Indian society.

Aymara   A people native to the Bolivian altiplano who were conquered by the Quechua Indians in the 15th century. Also one of the Indian peoples of contemporary Bolivia.

blanco   Spanish for "white"; used to designate a member of the white elite class of Bolivian society.

cholo   A city dweller of the lower class, most often of mixed Indian and Spanish heritage.

coca   A plant native to the Andean highlands of South America, the leaves of which are used to make cocaine, a drug with anesthetic properties. Traditionally, the Andean Indians chewed coca leaves to dull their pangs of hunger and withstand the frigid climate of the altiplano. Today, Bolivia is the second-largest producer of coca for the illegal drug trade.

diablada   A "devil dance" performed by elaborately costumed Indians; depicts the victory of good over evil.

encomiendas   The land grants issued to the Spanish conquistadores, giving them control over Indian labor and tribute as well as land. In return, the conquistadores were expected to introduce the Indians to the ways of Spanish society and to teach them the tenets of Roman Catholicism.

mestizo   A person of mixed Indian and European ancestry; sometimes used to refer specifically to middle-class Bolivians of mixed heritage.

mita   The obligatory contribution of labor periodically required of male Indians by both the Incas and the Spanish.

Movimiento Nacionalista Revolucionario (MNR)   The Nationalist Revolutionary Movement, a political party founded in 1941 that had as its goal the nationalization of Bolivia's primary industries. A central force in the revolution of 1952, the MNR governed Bolivia from 1952 to 1964 and is still a leading party.

Oriente   The easternmost and largest geographic region of Bolivia, constituting about two-thirds of the national territory. The Oriente is also known as the *llano*, or plain.

Quechua   Pronounced KAY-chwa. An Indian people, also known as the Inca, that conquered the Aymara in the 15th century; also one of Bolivia's contemporary Indian peoples.

rosca   The wealthy aristocracy that dominated Bolivian politics during the late 19th and early 20th centuries.

INDEX

PICTURE CREDITS

AP/Wide World Photos: pp. 46, 48, 76, 86; James Baker: p. 43; The Bettmann Archive: pp. 33, 40, 84, 88, 91, 97; Rob Cousins/Animals, Animals: p. 22; Courtesy Department Library Services, American Museum of Natural History: p. 34 (neg. # 331859); Michael Dick/Animals, Animals: p. 23; Jeffrey Foxx/United Nations: pp. 63, 74; Copyright Robert Frerck/Odyssey/Chicago: pp. 20, 66; John Isaac/United Nations: p. 58; Bejamin Porter: cover, pp. 2, 37, 38, 67, 68 (bottom), 69, 70–71, 72, 73, 79, 93, 96, 100; Gary Tong: pp. 6–7; United Nations: pp. 14, 16, 24, 53, 65, 68 (top), 70 (bottom), 80, 82, 85, 99, 102; UPI/Bettmann Archive: pp. 18, 28, 50, 55, 56, 104; Monica Von Thun-Calderón: p. 61